Be On Time!

By Catherine Ripley

CELEBRATION PRESS
Pearson Learning Group

Contents

Always Late or Have to Wait?

Are you always late for school? Do your friends and family often wait for you? Do you find yourself waiting for other people who are late?

If you are always late, you upset yourself and others. You have to rush and they have to wait. Waiting around is no fun.

When you are late, others have to wait for you.

What can you do to be on time? Read this book. It will help you to think about and plan your time. Then, you will not be late or make people wait for you. You can also share this book with people who make you wait.

If you plan your time, chances are that you will not be late.

People Count on You

Waiting for a friend or someone in your family is hard. You worry. You might think you have the wrong time. If the friend is always late, you might feel angry.

Your friends and family might feel this way too, if they have to wait for you. They count on you to be on time. So, being on time is a way to be nice to people.

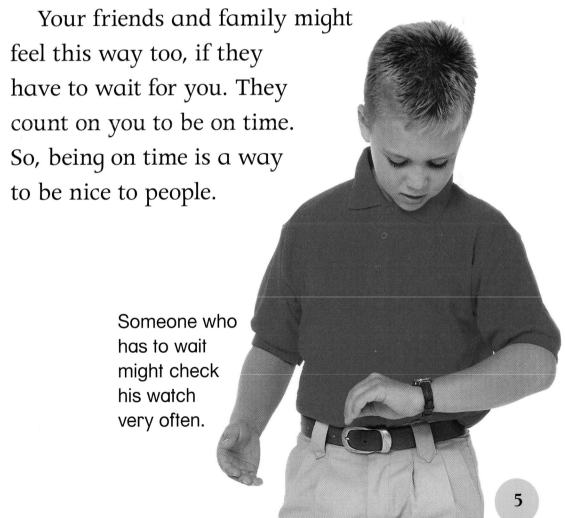

Someone who has to wait might check his watch very often.

What Can Happen if You Are Late

It isn't a good idea to be late. Why not? First, if you are late, you might miss an **event.** Your team might start a game without you. Your family might start dinner without you.

Second, being late can get you into trouble. For instance, you might have to pay a **fine** if you return a library book late.

You may have to pay a fine for returning books late to a library.

What Makes You Late?

There can be many reasons why you might be late. Maybe one morning you got ready for school in **record** time. Now, you think that short amount of time is all that you need to get ready. Yet most mornings you need more time.

Looking for things might make you late for school.

Early or Late?

You arrive at school at 5 minutes to 8:00. School starts at 8:00. Are you early or late?

You may be late because you try to do too much. For example, before going to a movie, you might try to finish your homework or walk the dog. These things take longer than you expect, so you are late getting to the movie.

How Long Does it Take?

Different **activities** take different amounts of time. Which activities below do you think take minutes to do? Which take hours?

- Brush your teeth.
- Feed the cat.
- Play soccer.
- Eat breakfast.
- Get dressed.
- Sleep at night.
- Make your bed.

When events take longer than you expect, you can be late for your next event.

Tips to Help You Be on Time

Being late all the time is a bad **habit**. If you want to change this habit, you need to plan your time better. There are tips that you can follow to **manage** your time better.

Take time to plan. Then, you will have a good idea of how much you can do.

Things to do	Time heeded
clean room	10 minutes
feed the dog	2 minutes
watch my favorite show	30 minutes
go to game	60 minutes
do homework	20 minutes

Tip 1: Find out how long it takes you to do something.

On the next school day, time yourself to see how long it takes to get ready for school. Subtract that amount of time from the time at which you are supposed to leave for school. This is the time that you should start getting ready for school every morning.

Time how long it takes you to get ready for school.

Get ready ahead of time.

Tip 2: Another tip to help you manage your time is to get your clothes ready at night. Lay them out on a chair. The next morning, you can put them on quickly. You won't spend time looking for something to wear.

Getting your clothes ready the night before will help you be on time.

Tip 3: Add extra time.

You never know when something **unexpected** may happen to make you late. So, add an extra 15 minutes to the time you need. Then if something does happen, you might still be on time.

Be prepared for unexpected things by adding extra time.

Tip 4:

Make a list.

Another tip is to make a list of what you have to do. Then, plan enough time for each activity. If there isn't enough time to do everything on your list, you may have to shorten your list.

A list will help you know if you have planned too many activities.

You Can Help Others

You can help others be on time, too. Share what you know about being on time. Tell your friends to plan ahead. Show them how to make a list of activities. Help members of your family time their activities. Then, not only will you be on time, everyone else will, too!

There are many sayings about time. Have you heard of these?
- Time waits for no one.
- Time is on your side.
- Time flies.
- Killing time.
- Time's up.
- Time out.
- Take your time.

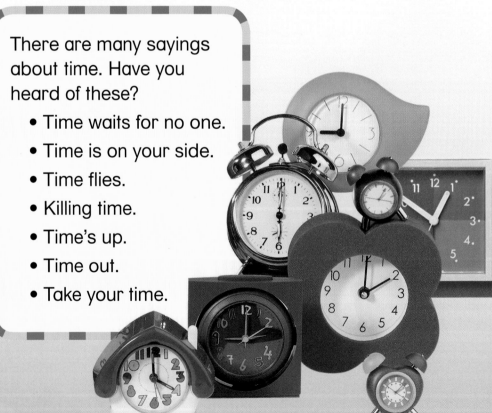

Glossary

activities	things to do
event	thing that happens
fine	a sum of money paid for breaking a rule
habit	something a person does over and over again
manage	to control or direct
record	the best speed yet reached
unexpected	not planned for

Index